# CANDLE MAKING BUSINESS

## THE GUIDE FOR BEGINNERS ON HOW TO MAKE HOMEMADE CANDLES IN 8 EASY STEPS AND MAKE MONEY FROM HOME

*Lorrie Paper*

# TABLE OF CONTENT

## Introduction

## PART 1 –How To Make Homemade Candles

*Chapter 1. Candle Making Tools*......................................................*11*

*Chapter 2. Candle Making Supplies (Raw Materials)*......................*23*

*Chapter 3. Steps To Making Candles*...............................................*33*

*Bonus For You. My Shopping Tips*...................................................*35*

*Chapter 4. Creative Candle Variations*...........................................*45*

## PART 2 – How To Start, Run & Grow Your New Business

*Chapter 5. Candle Making As A Business*.........................................*54*

*Chapter 6. The Candle Making Industry*...........................................*62*

*Chapter 7. Reasons You Should Start A Candle Making Business*........*67*

*Chapter 8. Essential Aspects Of Candle Making Business*...................*71*

*Chapter 9. Must Do's*.......................................................................*79*

*Chapter 10. Business Mistakes To Avoid*..........................................*87*

*Chapter 11. Promoting & Selling Your Candles Online*.....................*93*

*Chapter 12. Promoting & Selling Your Candles Offline*....................*97*

*Chapter 13. Selling Candles To Gift Shops*.....................................*102*

*Chapter 14. Weekly Plan To Start Your Business*.............................*106*

*Conclusion*....................................................................................*117*

# Introduction

This book about candle making business will teach you how you can start your own business making candles. This book will educate you on everything you would like to know to be able to start making candles and offering them.

This book is full of useful information that you need to know. This book will teach you everything from how to make candles down to how to market your candles. In case you need to create the candles yourself at that point, you may learn how to do that in this book.

This book will also tell you how to market your candles so that they are seen and sold. This is a simple and easy business that can bring in lots of money for you on the off chance that you are willing to work for it.

If you are looking for a simple and easy business that is profitable, then this book will educate you on everything you would like to know approximately candle making and selling candles for profit. You will be able to start your own candle-making business and earn an income from it.

The business will be very profitable if you are willing to work hard at it. You will be able to start your business by selling your candles online orthrough other means. You can create your own candles, or you can try to find wholesalers that have candle-making supplies. You will be able to create a variety of different types of scents as well.

*The book will also show you all methods of marketing your candles in various ways. This book will instruct you everything you would like to know almost this straightforward trade that will bring within the salary merely merit.*

*Candle making is easy to learn and can be a lot of fun. You will be able to make many different types of candles in this business, such as votive candles, pillar candles, taper candles, jar candles, scented candles, and more. You will also be able to shape your candles in many different ways as well. Making candles is a very simple business and can be a lot of fun. The business can also be profitable if you are willing to work hard at it.*

*Candle making is a simple and easy business that can bring in money for you if you are willing to work for it. Making candles can be done in the comfort of your own home as long as you have the right equipment. The book will teach you how to start your business.*

*This book is designed to help the candle-making hobbyist or the person who cannot afford to pay high prices for homemade candles. Making candles with a home-based candle-making business can be profitable if you are willing to work for it. This is a simple and easy business that does not require much capital. The book will also show you many methods of marketing your candles as well.*

*Making research before starting your candle business is a must. Candle making is a simple and easy business that is profitable if you are willing to work hard at it. You can also decide if you want to make your own candle-making supplies or if you want to use premade supplies. The book will show you how to market your candles in various ways. This book is designed to help the candle-making hobbyist or the person who cannot afford to pay high prices for homemade candles.*

*Candles have been around for centuries, and they are an awfully prevalent thing in our society nowadays. People can be seen buying candles for a variety of different reasons. Some people buy candles as gifts for their family members while others buy them to give to their vendors and friends to help them celebrate a special occasion. One of the foremost prevalent sorts of candles these days is the column candle due to its numerous incredible employments.*

*The pillar candle is a unique candle that has many uses, and it can also be very dangerous if you do not use it properly.*

*The pillar candle is a candle that was originally used to burn on the top of lit candelabra. The candle was made out of glass, and it was small enough so that it could be lit and hold up the candelabra. Today, there are many types of pillar candles made for different occasions such as weddings, Christmas, birthdays, and more. Pillar candles have many uses, and one of the most popular uses is for decoration in your house. Pillar candles are usually made out of metal, and they come in a variety of different colors. Some pillar candles alsocome in different shapes, such as hearts, bells, and more.*

# PART I

# How To Make Homemade Candles

# Chapter 1

# Candle Making Tools

## Awl

An awl is very useful for making holes for wicks in candles that have set hard.

## Bamboo Sticks

Bamboo sticks are handy for poking a hole through the candle when it is still soft for applying a wick.

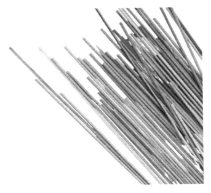

## Double Boiler

The double boiler uses water to heat the wax as melted wax can become quite volatile and will burn easily. To prevent this double boiler was invented the wax so can melt, and the temperatures could be controlled for easy use, and never exceed 100 °C. One can buy the professional candle-making kits and have the best from the very start, or you can make your own using a pan

with an aluminum jug in it so the wax will melt due to water boiling and hence never go over 100 °C.

## Professional Double Boiler

You can also use an electric frying pan with a kettle in it, and the kettle is very useful for pouring the wax where you want it.

# Electric Frying Pan

**I**     *Ensure your kettle will fit into the frying pan and then fill it with water and start boiling.*

# Kettle

**II**     *Place your wax in the kettle and monitor melting temperatures. The kettle gives you a very controlled pour, especially if you are making layered candles and do not want to splash.*

## Homemade Double Boiler

## Drill Bits

A drill bit can be used for cutting holes in the candle, which you then fill with colored wax for an effect like a dice candle.

## Glue Gun

We use the glue gun to fix a wick to the base of a container instead of using a sustainer plate which does not look good on the finished product.

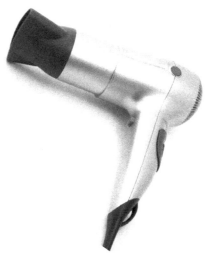

## Hair Drier

We use the hair drier to fix a tissue paper print onto the candle. Basically, we print the tissue, cut it to size then place it on the candle with wax paper on top. This wax paper we then heat up using the hair drier, and the wax melts into the tissue and covers the print with a layer of wax, and seals it into the candle.

## Hole cutters

The hole cutters are of varying sizes up to about 50mm and can be used for a variety of effects. They are not used in a drilling machine as the drill would be too strong for the wax, so hand drilling is better.

## Knife

The knife is used for cutting wax from a tray when making a spiral candle. The back of the knife is used for cleaning the candle and getting it to look smooth and clean.

## Pouring Pot

Once we have melted the wax, we need a jug-like utensil for pouring the wax into the molds, and this we call the pouring pot. It holds a good quantity of wax and can fill a reasonable number of molds with one pour. This makes the process quicker and handier. Again the cheaper alternative is an aluminum kettle approximately 3-4 liters in size for pouring the big candles.

## Palette Knife

The palette knife is used for waxing tissues to a candle via waxed paper, and it can be used for effects on softer candles.

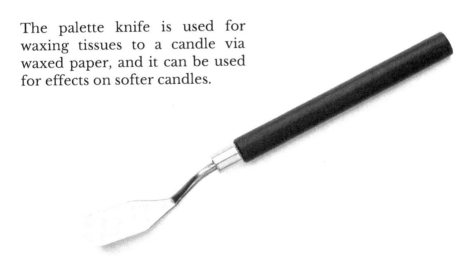

## Putty knife

The putty knife is used for lifting wax from a tray when you make a spiral or scroll candle.

## Scale

A scale is used to weigh each candle to determine how much wax has been used during the manufacturing process. This gives us an indication of the cost, so when we calculate all costs, we know how much wax we used, and it also allows us to find out how much wax we have left. Cover the scale with light paper to protect it from stains, and wax build-up.

## Small hacksaw

A small hacksaw is handy for cutting of excess pieces from a candle that has come out of a mold.

## Spoon

Some people use spoons for applying tissues to candles (which we will show you later) and also for dropping wax on to a surface for use in making candles with various layers of coloured waxes inside them.

## Square

This will be used for squaring off the base of your candle, particularly if you are making a spiral or scroll candle.

## Tape Measure

The tape has many uses for ensuring candle heights are correct or for measuring a homemade mold size etc..

## Thermometer

The glass thermometer is designed to clip onto the boiler and can be used to gauge the time when the wax will be ready for pouring. This thermometer sits in the wax and has to be cleaned frequently

## Glass Thermometer

The dial thermometer is sometimes called a candy or sugar thermometer but can be just as effective in wax as anywhere else. It uses a coil that expands or retracts as the temperature varies and is calibrated to give relatively accurate readings.

## Dial thermometer

The dial thermometer is sometimes called a candy or sugar thermometer but can be just as effective in wax as anywhere else.
It uses a coil which expands or retracts as the temperature varies and is calibrated to give relatively accurate readings.

## Digital Thermometer

The laser beam thermometer is about the best to have if you can find one, and they are not very expensive. You shine the laser onto the wax, and it gives an instant temperature and therefore helps in getting the wax to the correct temperature. The main advantage of this thermometer is it does not get dirty.

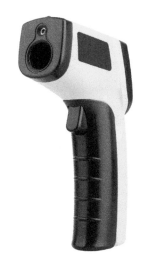

# Chapter 2

# Candle Making Supplies
## (Raw Materials)

## Choosing the Right Type of Wax for Your Candles

Over time, several types of wax were used to make candles. The first candle makers would use tallow to create candles, but it had many drawbacks (the most important one being the unpleasant smell that it brought upon when it burned). It was also fairly inefficient, and the light produced was dim; therefore, it did not allow the users to see much with it.

However, with the commercialization of candles, more and more materials came forward.

Nowadays, the most popular materials for candle making include:

## 1. Paraffin Wax

Paraffin wax is one of the most popular options because it is so inexpensive. Also referred to as straight wax, this does not have any additives in it, and it can also be used for different types of candles.

The advantage of paraffin is that it is fairly malleable. You can use it with a dipping technique, but you may also pour it into molds. It's a perfect base to make scented candles, colored candles, and fairly much any other type of candle.

One alternative to standard paraffin wax is also granulated wax. Used for crafting, this wax is made from 140° melt-point paraffin, which has been turned into beads. This wax does not have to be dissolved. You can simply pour it into a container and just insert the wick in the middle.

## 2. Soy Wax

Soy wax candles are also fairly popular, due to the fact that they are a 100% natural blend. Originating from hydrogenated soybeans, this type of oil is sold in several forms, soy wax flakes included. You may use it to create container candles, tarts, jarred candles, or whatever shape of candle you wish.

Soy wax and paraffin wax may be rather different when it comes to aspect and performance. For example, soy wax might need more dye compared to paraffin wax if you want to get the right color. On the plus side, soy wax will not depend so much on the temperature. Whereas paraffin wax will require particular temperature, soy wax is slightly more adaptable, which means the final product will be less affected.

## 3. Palm Wax

Once more, if you want to go all natural, then palm wax should be one of your top choices. Made using hydrogenating palm oil, palm wax allows you to make candles with unique textures.

In most cases, the wax forms a crystallized or feathering pattern on the surface of the candle, giving it a rather unique look.

When blended with soy wax, the result is rather smooth and "creamish".

There is also no unpleasant odor coming from this wax, making it perfect for scented candles and for decorative or therapeutic purposes.

## 4. Beeswax

Beeswax candles are also among the most popular options and considering that they have been around since the beginning of candle-making, this is understandable. They burn bright, and for a much longer time compared to other types of wax.

Compared to paraffin wax, beeswax is as natural as it can be. It's literally "goodness from the bees." Beeswax candles are environmentally-friendly and considering that they are devoid of chemicals, they are also very clean. For this reason, they can have an enticing floral aroma.

## 5. Gel Candle Wax

Most candle waxes have a solid color that you can barely see-through. However, if you want to go for more translucent candles, then gel should be your top choice. Mixing polymer resin and mineral oil, the glass resulted is translucent, and while it may not be exactly wax, it certainly acts like it.

People use gel wax due to its decorative purposes. For example, you may insert non-flammable items into it, making them appear embedded inside the case. You can also go for flower petals, from which the scent may also pour into the gel wax.

Overall, each type of wax will have its own benefits. Some waxes are suitable for certain types of candles, whereas others are better for other types. This is why you should know exactly the type of candle you want before deciding on the wax.

## Fragrance and/or Essential Oils

Some people buy candles just so that they could see the pretty lights dancing away in the darkness, creating a show of flickering flames. Still, aside from this benefit, other people use them for aromatherapy.

Do you have particular scents that you love smelling around? Maybe you love the smell of roses, or maybe you find the smell of lavender to be soothing. In any case, you may buy fragrance oils from a variety of places, and they are perfect to add to every candle.

However, the process may be quite complicated, and you must know precisely how you should use fragrance oils and essential oils. No, they are not the same thing, but you will find that out later on.

## Common Wax Additives

No candle wax is completely natural, and by simply reading the label, you can clearly distinguish a certain wax from its competitors. The additives will actually improve the quality of your candle, no matter if it's to increase its hardness or to promote the product's longevity.

Here are the most common additives that you will find in candle wax:

# Common Wax Additives

No candle wax is completely natural, and by simply reading the label, you can clearly distinguish a certain wax from its competitors. The additives will actually improve the quality of your candle, no matter if it's to increase its hardness or to promote the product's longevity.

Here are the most common additives that you will find in candle wax:

## Stearic Acid

Each time we hear "acid," our brain can't help but think about "caustic acid." However, stearic acid is nowhere close to that. To put it as simple as possible, stearic is made through the saponifying of the triglycerides into oils and fats using distillation and hot water.

Stearic acid is very common when it comes to candle-making, as it hardens the wax and prevents any slumping from occurring. For this reason, it is also used to make votive and pillar candles.

Plus, it will make a translucent wax slightly more opaque, retaining the fragrance and increasing the burn time.

When stearic acid is added, it will allow the wax to shrink during the cooling process. If you are planning to make candles in molds, this is actually a great additive to consider, as it facilitates the removal from the mold.

Most of the time, stearic acid is added to paraffin wax, and ideally, it should cover around 10-12% of the wax amount. If you are going for regular candles, 10% of stearic acid should be enough.

Otherwise, if you are opting for heavy use of fragrance oil, you should use around 12% stearic acid.

## Vybar

It may have a fancy name, but it is actually just an alternative to stearic acid. This additive is often referred to as "polymerized olefin" and can increase a candle's hardness, but without contributing to the brittleness that occasionally appears in candles.

This makes the candle soft, but not slumpy; thus, it is perfect if you wish to do some candle carving. Plus, like stearic acid, vybar also can increase the opacity of a candle and retain the fragrance. The melting point of the wax is also increased, meaning that the candles with this additive are likely to last for a much longer time.

For votive and pillar candles, you should get Vybar 103, whereas, for containers, you have to go for Vybar 260. There is also the option of Vybar 343 that has a more universal use.

## *UV Stabilizers*

If you are planning to keep your candles in the light, you might want to ensure your wax has UV stabilizers. This will stop them from losing color when they have been exposed to light, whether its UV rays or fluorescent lights.

Granted, a UV stabilizer will not prevent the fading of the color completely, but it will reduce it significantly, allowing your candle to look its best for a prolonged time. These additives also go under the name of UV protectant, UV absorbent, and UV inhibitor.

## Petrolatum

Petrolatum is generally used in the making of container candles, and it has the opposite effect of stearic acid and vybar.

This additive increases the oil content of the candle, making it creamier and easier to adhere to the containers. It is additionally a great choice if you're curious about candle carving and you need to have a wax that's marginally more moldable.

Petrolatum also decreases the shrinkage of the wax, so the chances are that the wax will harden just the way you pour it into the container. It also reduces the melting point of the candle, meaning that its burning time is also increased.

Depending on the wax that you buy, you might also come across other additives. These might include:

- *Microcrystalline Wax:* Used to harden the wax and extend its burning time. The melting point of the wax is also lowered.

- *Crisco Shortening:* It improves the scent throw of the candle.

- *Mineral Oil:* It leads to a mottling effect.

- *Polyabsorbate 80*: Mostly used when essential oils are involved, as it will prevent the oil from going down to the bottom of the candle.

Typically why you ought to be especially cautious when it comes to the added substances of a candle. You may see them as "chemicals," but they actually improve the behavior of your candle.

## Candle Wicks – How Do You Pick Them?

Just how you pick the candle wax, you need to be particularly attentive with the way you pick the candle wick. These strips of material are necessary to keep the flame, and without them, you can't really call the candle... well, "a candle."

In the beginning, hobbyists would make their own wicks. These days, you'll purchase them at a really reasonable cost, to the point that it's not indeed worth it to purchase string in arrange to form your claim wicks.

A wick will generally be attached to a metal wick tab. This is necessary to ensure that the flame won't burn through the container, therefore cracking the glass.

## Groups of Candle Wicks

Candle wicks are thrown into different categories, all suitable for different kinds of candles. They also have distinctive features that will behave distinctively with every burn. Here are the types of candle wicks that you will come across:

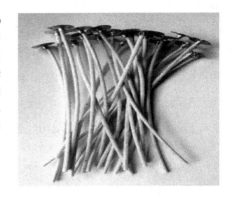

- *Flat Wicks*

Flat wicks are generally the most common kind. These are small threads that have been knitted or braided to form a bundle. The wicks are self-trimming, and as they burn, they will begin to curl. This type of wick is generally most suitable for pillar candles, tapers, and other free-standing types.

- *Cored Wicks*

Cored candle wicks are also braided, but they have a core material inside the knitted thread. Most of the time, it's made from cotton, paper, or zinc, practically anything that will help the wick stand in an upright manner. The recommendation is that you use them for votive, containers, or pillars, thanks to the rigidity of the neck.

- *Square Wicks*

A square wick will feature square tips, but rounded corners. Most of the time, it is used for beeswax candles, but it may also be used with pillar and taper candles. When a square wick burns, the tip will bend slightly.

- *Specialty Wicks*

A specialty wick will not fall into any category in particular, and is generally used for unique candles. Most of the time, you may see them in insect-repelling candles or oil lamps.

# My Shopping Tips

## Candle Make Tools

https://amzn.to/3u2bVjY

## Candle Making  Supplies

https://amzn.to/3u0tKQt

## Kit Candle Making Complet

https://amzn.to/3k4wrw5

https://amzn.to/2NpZcqB

# Chapter 3

# Steps To Making Candles

## The Four Main Processes

There are 4 main processes that you need to know in candle making. These processes may determine the consistency, strength, and burn time of your candle. Below is the list of the 4 essential processes:

- *Wax melting.* The wax needs to be correctly melted in order to produce strong and beautiful candles.

- *Wicking the candle.* Your wick may become submerged in the wax if you do not know how to place or hold the wick.

- *Pouring of the wax.* You may think that pouring of the wax does not require a technique or process, but it does. If you pour the wax wrongfully, your candles may have sinkholes near the wick. It may affect the strength and stability of your candles.

- *Curing.* This is the process of making the wax harden. You can cure the wax naturally by leaving it at room temperature overnight. Otherwise, you may put it within the ice chest or cooler. But, not all wax may be cured in the freezer or fridge.

# Melting the Wax

Determining the amount of wax needed. Before you could melt the wax, you may have to undergo an additional process. This is about how to determine how much wax you should melt. Candle-making kits have already pre-measured the wax you need. But, if you want to start making candles for business, you should familiarize yourself with this process.

This process will help you save some of your wax. Here are the steps:

1. Weigh your mold.
2. Fill your mold with water and take the weight.
3. Subtract the weight of the mold from the total weight of the mold and the water. The difference is the amount of wax you need.
4. Every pound of solid wax yield different amount of melted wax. Here is the approximate amount of each type of wax when melted:

- **Paraffin wax.** 1 pound can yield 18 to 20 ounces.
- **Soy wax.** 1 pound yields 16 ounces.
- **Beeswax.** 1 pound yields 14 ounces.
- **Palm wax.** 1 pound may yield 14 to 16 ounces.
- **Gel wax.** 1 pound may yield 16 ounces.

Below are the steps to follow when melting the wax through a double boiler.

1. Prepare two pots of different sizes.
2. Fill the bigger pot with water at around 1 inch deep. Put it over medium warmth and bring to a delicate bubble.
3. While you're holding up for the water to bubble, plan the amount of wax you would like.
4. Put it in the smaller pot. If you have a clip thermometer, or if you can clip your thermometer in the smaller pot, put it in.
5. After all the wax had totally melted, check its temperature. Make beyond any doubt that the temperature is at 180°F.

6. Turn off the stove and leave the wax to cool a little (about 90 to 135°) for the pouring process.

## Adding Additives and Wicking

Before the pouring process, there may be three steps that you need to do. These are adding fragrance and essential oils, wicking the candle, and decorating the candle.

*Adding Fragrance Oil*

Since fragrance oils can affect the consistency and stability of the wax, the process may overlap with the process of melting the wax. Here are the steps when adding the oil:

1. Decide how much fragrance oil you want to add or know how much oil is required by the recipe.
2. Determine the weight of the fragrance oil. Because of the different consistency, an ounce of oil and an ounce of melted wax may have different volume. Thus, base your additional wax on the weight of the oil and not according to its volume.
3. Prepare the same weight of wax and add it to the original amount of wax before proceeding with the melting process.
4. During the cooling period, prior to the pouring process, mix in your fragrance oil.
5. Proceed with the pouring process.

*Adding Essential Oils*

Essential oils are added before the pouring process. But you need to test the scent of the oil before the pouring process because some oils lose their scent or emit a foul scent when heated.

Here are the steps when adding essential oils:

1. After the wax had melted, add 10 drops of your desired essential oil to the wax. If the essential oil retains its smell, then wait for the pouring process.
2. If the essential oil does not retain its smell, you can add more drops of the essential oil to the wax until the wax becomes scented.
3. Let the wax cool a little for the pouring process.
4. After the wax had cooled, check if the scent remained. If it did, then proceed with the pouring process. If it did not, add a little more of the essential oil before pouring.

## Adding Herbs and spices

Since there are two ways of adding herbs in your candle, the steps for each may differ from each other.

### Adding Dry Herbs Directly to the Candle

1. If you are adding crushed dried herbs, you can add them directly to the wax after the cooling down period for the pouring process.
2. If you are adding spices, but you want the powder to be visible, add it before the pouring process. If you do not want it to be visible, add it after the wax had melted.
3. If you are adding herbs, spices, and dried flowers as side decors for pillars or votive candles, then you may have to do the following steps:

- After the wax had cooled a little, take a small amount of the wax.
- Brush the sides of your molds with the wax.
- Place the mold in the fridge for about a minute, or until the wax had set.
- Add another coat of wax. Arrange your herbs, dried leaves, or flowers at the side of your mold.
- Brush another coat of wax over the herbs. Repeat step 3.

- Wait for the pouring process.
- If you are adding spices, herbs, and flowers as a design for container candles, you may follow the stepsnmentioned above. But if you want them to have a floating effect, you may add them during the pouring process.

## *Adding herbal essences by infusion*

To infuse your candle with herbs, just add the herbal flowers, leaves, root, or bark in the oil after the melting process. Leave the herbs in the wax until it cools for the pouring process.
Strain the herbs before pouring the wax into the container or mold.

## *Adding Dyes*

The steps in adding essential oil to the candle are also the same for adding dyes. But, instead of the scent, the basis is the color of the wax.

## Wicking the Candle

There are two ways of wicking your candle. You can wick it using a wick pin and wick holder. But you can do without both.
If you are using wick pins and wick holders, you may follow these steps.

1. Attach your wick to the wick pin or tab. Place the wick with a pin at the center of your mold or container. For container candles, you may permanently attach the bottom end of the wick with a glue gun or candle round stickers.
2. Insert the other end of the wick to the wick holder.
3. Arrange the wick holder on the top of the mold or the container. Make sure that the wick is centered.
4. Pour the wax into the mold or container. Adjust the wick to the center.

5. Leave the wick holder until the wax hardens.
6. Slowly remove the wick holder and trim the excess wick.

If you are not using a pin or holder, you can wick your candle by using skewers or toothpicks as holder. But this process is only advisable for cored wicks or HTP series wicks.

The steps are simple. Just tie the wick in the skewer or toothpick. Place the improvised wick holder on top of the mold or the container. Make sure to pour the wax slowly so the wick will remain at the center.

## Pouring the wax

Except if you are adding designs to your candle, the steps in pouring the wax to your mold or container remain the same. Here are the steps:

1. After the wax had melted, cool your wax until the temperature drops to around 90 to 135°. You have to let your wax cool down, or it will make your wax float.
2. Give the wax a slow stir to burst any bubbles.
3. Pour the wax into the container. In pouring, start at the center or near the wick, especially if you are using an unwaxed wick. The wick will absorb the wax near it and may result in a sinkhole in the middle.
4. Fill the mold or the container up to three-fourths of its height.
5. Lightly cure the candle by leaving it at room temperature for four hours or by putting it in the fridge for at least an hour. Do not freeze the wax, or else, the wax will not sink and will not cover possible sinkholes.
6. After the light cure, reheat the remaining wax. Pour it on top of the hardened candle until you covered the mold or the desired limit for the container.
7. Let the candle cure at room temperature for at least 8 hours before lighting it.

## Curing the Candle

The curing process only has one step, and that is to leave the candle for at least 8 hours at room temperature. Some candles may require a longer curing period.
There is also a process of fast cure. This is putting the newly poured candle in the fridge to cure faster.

## Removing the Candle from the Mold

If you are using a reusable mold, one challenge that you may encounter is removing the candles from the mold. Incorrect unmolding may result in cracked or broken candles. Two steps can make it easy for you to overcome this hurdle. The first one is seasoning your mold, and the other is shrinking the wax.

- *Seasoning.* This is the process of making the mold in tune with the wax you are using. This could mean that you may have to use a specific mold for every wax you use. This process can take a while, too.

To season your mold, just melt the wax and pour it into the mold. Let the wax harden. Take out the hardened wax from the mold. You may notice that some bits of the wax may be left behind, or the wax will have some dent.
Melt the wax again and pour it back to the mold. Then repeat the previous step.
Continue to repeat the steps until the wax comes out clean and almost perfect. This will presently make it less demanding for you to unmold your candles. Taking the candle carefully out of the mold

- *Shrinking.* It is the process of shrinking the candle in the fridge or freezer.

If the candle would not slip out of the mold, do not tap the mold. You may dent or break the wax. Instead, place the mold in the fridge for five minutes or in the freezer for a minute.

The wax will shrink, and the candle will become smaller. It will slip easily out of the mold.

# Chapter 4

# Creative Candle Variations

## Floral Candles

Floral candles are a fairly common sight in homes and workplaces. These candles are used to add a floral scent to the home and are often made from natural materials like roses, lilacs, and petals of many other flowers. These candles are known to have several benefits. Here are 6 surprising benefits of using floral candles.

### 1. It aids in healing cuts and wounds naturally

Natural rose petal candles are known to aid in healing wounds, cuts, and burns naturally. A study

performed on rats showed that burns in rats healed faster when they were exposed to rose petal extract for a few days than those who did not receive the treatment. This shows that floral candles can help our body recover from minor injuries quickly.

## 2. Improves nervous system disorders

Floral candles make it easy to inhale an essential oil for any kind of disorder or disease that is related to the nervous system. The essential oils taken from flowers and plants can help ease cramps in muscles, stiff joints, and muscle spasms.

## 3. Support immune system

Floral candles have a natural ability to strengthen and aid in repairing the immune system. The essential oils found in a rose candle stimulate the production of white blood cells that help combat infection and promote healing of wounds. Essential oils can also improve sleep patterns of people with insomnia problems, reducing fatigue experienced while falling asleep. This can be achieved by inhaling the scent of flowers for 20 minutes before bedtime.

## 4. Fight against cancer and other diseases

There are several types of flowers that can help fight against cancer and other diseases. Lavender has anti-inflammatory, analgesic; anticonvulsant, antioxidant, and antimicrobial properties that help the body fight any type of disease.

## 5. Relaxation during meditation

Using floral candles during meditation can help achieve a deep state of relaxation. The scent of the candle helps clear one's mind from any kind of distractions. Using floral candles during meditation can give an individual greater access to achieving inner peace. The floral candles also aid in boosting concentration which is necessary for achieving one's goals in life through meditation.

Floral candles can improve your focus and concentration. The essential oils mixed in the rose petals can help decrease anxiety levels while increasing feelings of relaxation and calmness.

Floral candles can be added to an office environment that promotes relaxation. These candles can create a relaxing mood in a workplace to help reduce stress levels among the employees.

## Colorful Candles

Colorful candles are used in our daily life. We use candles for many purposes in our daily life. Colorful candles have been in use from the ancient days where they were used as a source of light. As technology advanced, the production and marketing of colorful candles also changed. They are presently accessible in numerous shapes, sizes, and colors. A decorative candle holder is another important thing to be kept in mind while buying colorful light candles.

The color of the candle is determined by its kind, material, and form. Each type of colored candle has a unique color. The colors also change according to their region. For example, a yellow candle has different shades and colors in India as compared to other countries or regions.

The importance of colors is growing day by day. Colors play a very important role in life. It gives a positive feeling of joy and happiness to our hearts while looking at colorful things. Many kinds of candles are available today according to our need, for example, colored pillar candles, colored votive candles, and colored tea light candles.

The colorful candle is used as a decoration object in homes and public places such as hotels and restaurants, etc., where we use candle holders for better appeal and illumination.

Candles are already in use for a long time, but still, they are in trend. In everyday life, we see color candles lightened and used for decoration purposes. Colorful candles are combined with some other things such as candle holders, ceramic holders, etc..

The colorful candle is a very important thing which we use in our daily life. And also they have a great value of color in them which gives us a very good feeling. They are used at home for personal and decorative purposes and at public places like hotels, restaurants, and schools, etc., where they are placed on the table or the wall to light up the place as well as to decorate the surroundings. Some color candles are lighted up with the help of regular electric bulbs, but many have candles with unique shapes of their own.

The colorful candle is a very helpful thing, and it is also used for decoration purposes. It can be used in households, offices, schools, hospitals, and many other places. It can be used for making special things like birthday cakes, decoration purposes, etc., as well as to save money by not burning fuel to light them up. It is made up of very easily available things. It is made up of wax and wicks which are woven into a string and then fixed in the holder to give a pleasant look. The colorfulness of the candle also provides an additional hue to the surroundings, which makes them very friendly for human eyes.

Colorful candles are also used as decorative accessories for parties, house warming's, etc., along with decorative items such as flowers, wall hangings, etc., or just used on their own to lighten up dark corners and gardens as well as giving a warm glow when sitting outside in the evenings. Candles may seem like an old thing, but they are still widely used by all classes of people today. Many people prefer to use colorful candles over other things like fluorescent lights and electric lights because candles give a subtle glow to the surroundings, which can't be seen with other light sources.

The majority of white and black colored candles are used in factories, offices, hotels, and restaurants. While using them, people should also remember that these colors might be harmful to the eyes. In order to protect the eyes, the worker should not look directly into the flame of a candle while working as it will cause strain on the eyes. Many people often think that they can use colorful candles for light instead of regular white-black colored candles, but it is not actually true. Colored candles are generally used in case of emergency, but regular white-black colored candles should be used only in suitable places where they will not be harmful to human health and eyesight.

Still, colored candles are widely used in many countries as the light of those candles is warm and soothing. Many candle makers all over the world specialize in the production of colored candles. Different countries have their own types of colored candles, which are different from each other.

Colored candles produce various colors depending on how they are made and the composition used to make them. However, it can be said that most colored candles look more beautiful when they are made with pillar wax instead of using regular thin wicks. Pillar wax is generallyused because it produces the brightest light and color combination out of all the other combinations as well as it gives room for maximum dispersion of color in the darkness.

## Buried treasure candles

Buried treasure candles are an interesting concept. These are candles that are burned for a certain length of time to release the scent of whatever treasure you want. The longer the candle is burned, the stronger the smell. This is a fairly unique idea, and has been in existence for quite some time. It goes to show that sometimes the simplest of ideas can be the most effective.

A buried treasure candle is a simple product, but it contains many wonderful features. This special candle creates a unique atmosphere that will add to any special occasion. Rather than simply setting out a few candles for lighting during your special event, why not

burn one that will release the smell of whatever treasure you want? The longer the candle is burned, the stronger that scent will become. You can find pirate and pirate ship candles as well as hidden cave scents and countless others.

The possibilities here are endless!

These candles are not quite like any others on the market right now. They do not come in an opaque jar, as is the case with most candles. Instead, they come in a clear jar. This is just another way to say that you will not be able to see what is inside the candle until you open it up. The candle itself will contain multiple scents and many other features that create the perfect experience. It may feel a small bizarre to be opening up something you did not arrange, but it is totally suitable to do so!

You may be wondering if these candles really have any power. Will the scent actually permeate through your home and create an exotic atmosphere? Will you be able to smell it? These are very good questions that you should consider before purchasing this product. Your goal is to create a positive experience for yourself, as well as for others in your home. Be beyond any doubt to keep this in intellect once you are purchasing these candles, and don't be afraid to pay a small additional for the most!

You may have just discovered the best thing since sliced bread. Buried treasure candles are an interesting concept that has been around for quite some time. The unique bottles are intriguing in and of themselves, but the scents should leave you very impressed. Anyone who walks into your home will be amazed by how good it smells. These candles have a lot of power, and they will definitely make an impression.

# PART II

# How To Start, Run & Grow Your New Business

# Chapter 5

# Candle Making As A Business

## From hobby to business

Candle making can be a very cheap business to set up compared to other manufacturing types because the raw material cost is affordable. Even the equipment cost is not very expensive.

Of course, the size of the business you want to set up will determine the ultimate setup cost. You will need to review all aspects of setting up a business, and then make up a Startup Budget to precisely know the financial commitments.

When you have that figure, you then need to ensure you have the money to set up. But don't be fooled by thinking that is the end of it. Most businesses do not turn a profit until 9 months, or even more realistically, up to two years. So you need to make sure you have funds to carry you through for that time and extra equipment and materials as the business grows.

Let's look at setting up a business, whether on commercial premises or a home-based business. There is not much difference in what needs to be researched except that if it is to be on commercial premises, then a lease and associated costs will need to be taken into account.

When starting a business, you really need to have thought about who your ideal client is and target them with your products. If you complete a business plan, you will have answered many questions about your business that you may not have thought of, including finance, competition, product range, marketing, and other factors related to operating a business. Here is a link to download a FREE business plan template. You will find many doubts have been alleviated when you do this plan, and you will have a much clearer idea about the overall business you want to start.

A few issues ought to be checked out sometime recently you spend cash on setting up your trade. Not all local authorities allow home businesses of all types, and candle making does use flammable products, so you need to check that you are not going to be fined for doing something that you should not be doing.

Here is an **essential checklist** when starting a new business:

- ☑ Check with the local authorities and see that you are not contravening any local by-laws with a candle-making business.

- ☑ Talk to your accountant and register a business name, this can be your name for tax purposes, but for trading purposes, you might want to write a business name as well, organize a bookkeeper if necessary.

- ☑ Set up a business bank account and make sure it has a visa card to go with it, this could be a credit card or a debit visa card, whichever you prefer, it is much easier and cheaper to do your accounts at the end of the year if you have separate financial records for your business transactions.

- ☑ Organize a credit card payment system for customer purchases, face to face, internet, and by phone.

- ☑ Set up an online payment system such as PayPal or one of the other online payment gateways such as 1ShoppingCart, Product Pay, etc.

- ✓ Price and order your stationery and packaging.

- ✓ Set up an area at home where you are going to work and get it ready or organize leased premises.

- ✓ Make sure you have completed your business plan and a marketing plan for 12 months.

- ✓ Get your insurances organized.

- ✓ Buy your equipment and raw materials or whatever it is you need to do business and store them safely.

- ✓ Plan a launch of your business.

## Insurance

Insurance is a risk management strategy that business owners seriously need to consider. If you are employing staff, producing a product, or have the public visiting your premises, it is folly not to protect yourself in this litigious society that we live in.

Insurance is a tax-deductible expense against the business.

There are several insurances that a business owner needs to consider, and they are:

- Public liability insurance
- Loss of income insurance
- Asset insurance
- Vehicle insurance
- Errors and omissions liability
- insurance if contracting staff

There are different names for some of the insurance covers with the different companies, but essentially, they are similar so it is just a matter of finding the one that suits your purpose.

## Public Liability Insurance

A business may not need all of the insurances listed above, but one that is a must, in my view, is public liability insurance (orgeneral liability insurance, or commercial general liability insurance). This protection covers a commerce proprietor for such things as a client mishap at the premises, or any other substantial hurt caused at the premises, by an item made by the commerce or at an offering location such as a slow down or a has house amid a party introduction.

## Loss of Income Insurance

This is excellent insurance for anyone who has a good income and financial commitments, but may be difficult to get until you have proven income, usually 2 years tax figures. As far as a one-person business is concerned, if the owner should have an accident or suffers an illness that incapacitates them for some time, they may be able to claim against their insurance to cover their income.
There are different levels with this insurance, so what you receive, when it starts, and how long it will last will be determined by the level of cover taken out.

## Asset Insurance (Property Insurance)

This is not a difficult one to understand. If you have expensive equipment in your business, you will most likely want to cover it for theft, breakdown, and possible damage. It will protect your office furniture and equipment, your manufacturing equipment, and any other items that you use to make your business happen.

## Vehicle Insurance

This can be a tricky one, and you may need to check out how this works with your insurance company because it will come down to ownership and usage. You may need to talk to your accountant about this one.

*Errors and Omissions Liability Insurance*

This particular insurance relates to a business where forms and contracts are used and could apply if you have contract sellers or candle makers.

## Operations

All home businesses need to be set up professionally and need to have a designated phone line, whether it is landline or mobile, which is of no consequence today.

You need to have a business website (either as a blog or a static site selling your products) and all the usual business stationery of business cards, packaging, business letterheads, flyers, and price lists. It is easy enough to put something out from the computer if you so, wish and that can be a good start.

You need to decide how you will get around the situations where you have to meet clients if this applies to your business. If you do not have an appropriate space at home, you can arrange to meet in a café or like this is quite acceptable.

## Commercial Premises

A commercial lease needs to be signed for those who want to have either a reasonable-sized manufacturing candle-makingbbusiness or a manufacturing and retail business from the same premises. There are several things to take into account here:

1. Commercial premises are valued by location, amongst other things.
2. When manufacturing from the same premise's consideration has to be given to the area required and the lease cost to see if it is economical.
3. Retail businesses do need good exposure, so you may need to know if it is worth having one premise for both areas of the company or two premises, one for retail and one for manufacturing.

4. Take care not to lock yourself into a long lease for the first term, you need to discuss with your solicitor your obligations as a lessee.

## Creating A Product Range

As you will be aware, there is a wide range of candles that you can make, and because of that, you will have to make some decisions. Research and see how you can make your candles or presentation (boxing, etc.) different from your competitors.
This means that you are going to have to decide on your range so that you can:

- Order the required raw materials
- Cost the making of each item
- Find out which candles are selling in your area
- Order packaging and labeling

When selling products, the idea is to sell a cluster of ranges. So, in other words, you may carry 9 full ranges. These 9 ranges may be made up this way: 3 herbal fragrances, 2 flower fragrances, 2 musk fragrances, and 2 homeopathic fragrances. Or you may want to specialize in a certain way, say only make homeopathy candles, and that is alright too. But you want to have a selection of fragrances and shapes.

I am not sure if you are aware of how marketing and display of products are done, but they are called 'stories' as there is a likeness which shows throughout the whole range. Here is an example of how you might set up a story:

*Rose Bud Candles (pink candles with a rose fragrance – 33 in total)*
*12 x votive candles*
*6 x 3 inch ball candles*
*3 x 6 inch round pillar candles*
*6 x 9 inch round pillar candles*
*3 x 3 inch square pillar candles*
*3 x 6 inch square pillar candles*

*33 in total*

If you had 9 different colors and fragrances on display like this, then you would have a very attractive display. It would be 297 candles in total. That is a lot of candles, and you may only start out with 5 different types and change one or two throughout the year.

# Chapter 6

# The Candle Making Industry

## Market Capitalization

Market Capitalization in candle-making business is measured by calculating the price times the number of shares outstanding. This is determined by using the company's stock price and the number of shares floated in the market. An increase in the company's market capitalization indicates to investors that the company is heading in a positive direction by seeing a growth in its businesses' value. This growth in value shows investors that other people also believe that there is a potential for future profits and increased sales. Thus, it is a way of showing investors through company value how much they think the share price should be. The higher the amount it's valued at, the more investors believe in the company than others do. Thus it gives them more confidence to invest their money into it as a source of income.

Since the most common use of candles is during home gatherings, they market mainly to homeowners looking for decorations for their homes, weddings, parties, or any other occasion. This is important because, as candle makers, we know that there's a high chance a candle will be purchased at least once every year. This means that every year one person in each household will buy an average of 2-3 candles, in some cases even more than 5.

Therefore, market trends have shown us that there is potential for an increase in employment, increasing our revenue and profits in the long term, as the bigger businesses are hiring more employees and thus increasing production.

## Revenue and Earnings

The trend of light sources is changing. This is why the demand for candles has been increasing noticeably. The number of U.S. households using candles has risen by 10% between 2011 and 2012. More than half of all U.S. households use candles regularly. The use of candle-making products has increased by 5% in 2012 alone. The U.S. candle-making market was valued at $2.4 billion in 2012, with an increase of 6% compared to 2011.

The U.S. candle-making industry is composed of approximately 2,500 manufacturers employing more than 10,000 people. The candle vendors are mainly based in the Southern US. The leading companies have headquarters in New Jersey and Pennsylvania.

Candles are found in many homes across America. As a result of this popularity, the candle-making industry has grown considerably. The U.S. is among the top three countries by volume for candles being produced every year.

In 2012, the U.S. candle-making industry was valued at $2.4 billion, with a 5% increase in 2012 compared to 2011.
Candles are used in many holiday celebrations such as Christmas, Valentine's Day, and Easter. People use candles to decorate the house for these holidays and on opposite dates such as New Year's Eve, July 4th, and Halloween. Candles may also be used in other ways, such as to give out fragrances or burn food items during various feasts and parties.
This is why the candle-making industry can be seen to flourish in the country at all times of the year.

# Training Employees

To provide good customer service, you need to make sure that every employee within your business is trained and knows what to do. Consider how you can train employees once you hire them.

It is essential to realize that when selling soaps and candles, all employees need to be in sales, and you should only hire those who can provide excellent customer service, no matter what position they are placed in. You want to create a business culture where all employees help the customers no matter what they are doing.

It would help if you chose to hire employees who have a caring attitude, are patient, and listen, empathize, ask appropriate questions, and are good at problem-solving. Remember, you are hiring a face and voice for your company.
The first thing you need to teach new employees is how to interact with customers. Do some role-playing so they can practice their new skills. Employees need to learn to empathize, apologize, and defuse a situation when dealing with upset customers.

Your employees need to be trained to genuinely listen to customers and adapt their approach to each situation. Their speaking style should be casual-yet-professional: contractions, short sentences, and a light tone of voice. They need to warm up interaction with customers and help build a relationship with a customer who has a question or minor concern that can be easily resolved. However, they also need to be aware of when to become more formal and serious if customers are angry or extremely frustrated and aren't able to get exactly what they want. It is best to teach employees easy-to-remember techniques to rely on during stressful situations.

Some several companies and organizations can help take your customer service training to the next level. If needed, consider sending critical employees to in-person training seminars or bring in a professional to train your entire staff.

It would offer assistance in case you attempted to illuminate client benefit issues before your representatives to appear them how to do it. If you have someone really good at customer service, then ask them to help you teach the others.

You should occasionally work near those who work closely with the customers. This way, you can offer on-the-spot training and offer suggestions on alternate ways to deal with customers' issues.

# Chapter 7

# Reasons You Should Start A Candle Making Business

## Why should you Make Your Candles?

If you're still pondering about giving a candle, having a shot, or not, then reading through the list below may help you make a decision.

Making candles may be an operation of profit and fulfillment. Candles are lovely to have on hand for several occasions, making them flexible and functional home decor pieces, let alone valuable resources in case of an electrical outage. Candle-making can be enjoyable and entertaining, so there are many advantages to this until you know the technique and do so.

1. *You can widen your creativity!*

With each passing year, the effects of fun aromatic environments are more apparent. It is not aromatherapy, but candle therapy, a blend of two senses to establish an unrivaled feeling of well-being and absolute joy.

Creating your candles is easy; it takes very little time; it uses only products you already have at home so that it will have the environmental effect (in terms of packaging, so transport costs). Ultimately, you have an element that is you in terms of scents and colors, beautifully matching your house.

They should not ignore the benefits of distinct smells. In the end, you have an item, which is wholly you in terms of aromas and colors, blending perfectly with your home. We should not overlook the benefits of distinctive aromas. You'll find one that renders relaxation almost compulsive, another one that follows fine dining and pictures the fire that invites your partner home to the hope of a passionate night?

You may render your candles as straightforward or complicated as you like them to be. There's no doubt about what you'll and can't do for candles made by you. Indeed, some of your concepts might not be as well as you might have liked, but they help you know and develop with the next ones!

The numerous methods out there when it comes to producing different candle styles are infinite and are still that and improving to this day.

2. *Make Money*

Not as it was that, you just will save money, but by creating your candles, you'll be able to gain cash as well. Setting up a home-based candle company will assist you to boost your profit when doing something you appreciate. On the off chance that trade seems too vast and complex, you'll begin by facilitating a candle-stall at fairs and community occasions. You'll dispatch a web store running from your domestic claim without having any additional room or cash. Scented candles, plan candles, and uncommonly shaped candles are a few of the recommendations that the swarms will bring in.
Candles are utilized amid the year, and tireless requests for handcrafted candles will be shown.

### 3. *Know Accurately What Fixings Are Going Into Your Candlemaking*

The increasingly growing issues about using environmentally sustainable and safe materials in products around us make the candles an even better choice. Some of the candle makers have adjusted to the evolving times and use certain additives more often today, but you will never say with certainty until you try it yourself.

### 4. *Creating Your Scent Combinations or Choosing Your Fragrances*

This point can go hand and hand with the previous one, but I believe it merits its spot on the list.
Two people will not have similar likes when it comes to the smell of a candle. The fragrances' strength is also one of the reasons that can trigger the most important differences of opinion among all lovers of candles. Many people enjoy candles that are so strong they can spread the scent around a whole space just before they're even lit, while others like it when you can only get faint traces of scent here and there. Candle manufacturers are unable to satisfy all needs, so producing their candles is a perfect opportunity for experimentation. Do you have a smell you would like to go after? Please think of the primary ingredients that make it, and check variations of scent oils to build it.

### 5. *They are simple to make and fun!*

It is as easy as restocking and getting one of the products you just finished using! You will seem like a professional in no time.

### 6. *Save Money*

Making handmade candles is a perfect way to save money. You not only won't need to purchase the candles, but you will still save money on friends and family presents. Buying bulk supplies would help you save money on the raw materials you require for this project.

# Chapter 8

# Essential Aspects Of Candle Making Business

## You Need to Conduct Market Research

Before starting your business, you probably heard about market research and assumed it was just for larger enterprises.
However, conducting market research can also help small businesses like your home-based one. Remember that when it comes to business, knowledge is power. No matter what you are selling, it is essential to understand the market you're working within.

The only difference is that larger businesses can do market research that can be costly. They have entire teams focused only on interviewing customers, conducting surveys, holding focus groups, and analyzing customers' patterns. As a small business, you have a smaller budget; but you'll still be able to carry out useful market research.
So just why am I telling you to do this before starting your business?

## Why Conduct Market Research

A few different times within your company's business have market research done that can be very useful. Consider some of the benefit areas:

**It can help you to determine if a new business idea is viable:** Say you have an idea for starting a new candle line or a new type of soap; do you know if there is a market for it and whether or not it will sell? It would help if you didn't guess since you could end up losing a lot of money; instead, you can use market research to find out before making money and time investment.

**Marketing research is also helpful if you plan to move into new markets:** This can be important if you start planning to sell abroad. Countries and cultures are different and have their own markets. What works for your business in the United States may not work in Canada. Market research will help you determine the difference and prepare to make the necessary adaptations.

**Market research is vital if you plan to launch a new product or service:** You may think your soaps and candles are selling great, but maybe your customers have a different idea. Before launching your business, you should make sure you get feedback to make any necessary changes.

In conclusion, advertise inquire about is vital in case you wish to apply for trade financing. On the off chance that you'll show potential speculators that there's a hole within the advertise which your trade can fill it, at that point you'll have distant better; a much better; a higher; a healthier; an improved, and a higher chance of getting affirmed for financing.

## Focus Your Market Research

On the off chance merely have to conduct exhibit request, the first vital thing to be past any question is keeping it solidly controlled.

Concentrate as it were on the critical zones that matter to your commerce. To do this, develop a list of many fundamental questions you need to know and, after that, decide the data you wish in arrange to urge answers to these questions.

From here, you can determine how best to get these answers. Perhaps it is through a focus group, online research, or survey. Don't fall into the trap of asking a lot of additional questions. If you stay focused and on topic, you'll get helpful answers that will allow you to adjust your business strategy as needed.

## Six Tips to Effective Market Research

1. If you       need to urge the foremost out of your little commerce showcase investigate, at that point, there are five things I've learned that can best assist you have victory.
2. Start your market research as early as possible. Whether you plan to sell locally or globally, knowing your potential size of growth is critical. Do your research before launching your business or breaking into any new markets.
3. Make sure you don't waste money. As a small business, you don't have a lot to spare for expensive research. A practical and inexpensive option is to use small focus groups and surveys from your existing customers.
4. If you don't have customers who are already buying your soaps and candles in small batches, you can look for existing research. Soaps and candles are a big market, and the chances are that someone has already done the market research you need. So look for online reports, field reviews, or magazine articles that may discuss your areas.
5. It is essential to determine what your customers are saying. The internet is a great way to find out what potential customers may think. Read consumer blogs, watch YouTube videos, browse discussion forums or other social media to see what people are saying, and know where to focus your business efforts.
6. Lastly, you can use the data from the larger businesses that have the money to spend. Google is a prime example of a company that consumes large amounts of money to collect research. Look at Google Trends and Google customer surveys

to see what people are looking for, and then you can evaluate if there is a gap that you can fill. These findings are often free, and you can take advantage of them.

## Don't Expect Too Much

Market research helps provide you with information about your target market, but it won't predict the success of your business with any great accuracy. This is because of four key things you need to remember when conducting market research and what you expect to get from it:

- A small sampling of potential customers may not represent the entire market.
- People may not say what they truly believe in surveys.
- Research may not focus on new trends.
- How your business acts within the market can have an impact on the outcome.

This isn't to say you shouldn't conduct market research. It is meant to tell you that you should use the results as a guideline and not a rule on where to take your business. It is best to rely on your gut instincts since they come from years of experience working in the field and seeing what happens.

It will help you to see if there is a market demand for your products or services. It won't help you see if your business will succeed, but it will help you get insights into opportunities you can use to increase business sales. When you combine market research with your own intuition and customer feedback once you launch, then you'll be able to grow your business successfully.

Along with market research, it is also a good idea to define your target market before you launch your business. This way, you know just who you want to focus your efforts on, and this can be something you learn through market research.

# You Need to Define Your Target Market

One of the steps you need to take before launching your business is to define your target market. This is often a large step, and sometimes you'll need to ask for help. So let's consider a target market, why it is important to know it, and how to establish one for your business.

## Target Market Definition

Many new business owners mistake a target market for their current customers or people like them as their target market.
However, these aren't necessarily going to be the right people. A target market is focused more on a particular group of potential customers. It looks at the people you want to market to sell more of your products. The target market needs to be so specific that you can picture unique individuals.

The target market is key to your business's success. Knowing this target market and knowing it intimately can make or break a new business. Your target market will define your product line; show you where to focus on wholesale efforts and how you will create advertisements and market campaigns. This is why you need a specific target market because you need to fill their needs, and you can only do this by knowing how they think.

However, keep in mind that having a defined target market doesn't mean you need to put up a barrier to other options. Just because someone doesn't meet your target market doesn't mean they won't still buy your products or services. However, it simply means you should let someone outside your target market define the choices you make for your business. Let's consider the benefits of defining your target market before launching your business.

# The Benefits of a Target Market

When you have a clear vision of your target market, you will be increasing the chances of having a successful business.
When you define your target market, you'll be able to do five things:

1. You'll be able to see if there are enough potential customers for you to start your business. You'll be able to know if there is enough demand for your products.
2. You'll be able to adjust your business idea to meet the needs of your potential customers to increase your chances of success from the start of your business.
3. Be able to tailor your products to meet your customers' needs and desires, making them more likely to purchase.
4. You'll be able to target your marketing efforts in order to reach the most promising potential clients.
5. You'll be able to craft a marketing message that has the right tone, language, and attitude to appeal to your potential customers.

It is important to also know what a target market won't do. For starters, it won't limit your business. People who are first starting a business tend to avoid a target market because they feel it restricts their business or reduces the number of sales they can have. This can be a major misguided judgment that can lead to disappointment. If you simply open your business to anyone and everyone, then you won't know where to focus your efforts, and you'll take on too much for too little return. Rather you can make a targeted effort, and once you succeed, you can start expanding to other areas and markets.

Secondly, when you have a target market in place, you'll be able to increase your cost efficiency. Unless you have unlimited resources, you want to focus your marketing efforts on those who are most likely to purchase your products. This way, you won't waste your precious time and money as you start up a new business.

## Picking Your Target Market

There are lot of strategies you'll be able utilize to select your target showcase. You can use all the methods to help narrow your focus. The goal of picking a target market is to define the ideal customers. It should be one that can both support your business, but also be someone you can relate to. Let's look at the steps you can use to find your target market.

## Suppliers

Wax is heavy and costly to ship. Therefore, it is economical to have a local supplier. Your craft shop is the place to start. However, if it cannot fill your needs, ask the manager for the names and addresses of local wholesale suppliers who sell to individuals. Also, check your yellow pages. Here are some regional suppliers:

| Northwest | South | Midwest |
|---|---|---|
| Barker Candle Supplies | Earth Guild | The CandleMaker |
| (800) 543-0601 | (800) 327-8448 | (888) 251-4618 |
| | www.earthguild.com | www.thecandlemaker.com |

| Northeast | West Coast |
|---|---|
| The Candle Mill | Yaley Enterprises Inc. |
| (800) 772-3759 | (877) 365-5212 |
| | www.yaley.com |

# *Chapter 9*

# *Must Do's*

## You Need to Develop a Brand

You need to create and implement a clear business brand that allows you to earn credibility, set customer expectations, make clear the purpose and values of the business, help the business stand out from the competition, and more. Many positives come from good branding, and you need to make sure your business is well branded before you get started selling products.

All businesses need a positive brand to succeed and have a strong future. Branding would be easy if all you had to do was put a logo on the product. However, branding is about more than this. Think of your brand as what customers, employees, and others think about your company. Your business brand is basically the same as a personality for your business. It is the ideals, beliefs, and values that the business projects to the rest of the world.

You need to carefully think about your brand before you launch your business. It is never too late to consider branding your business, but it will be more effective to do it before launching your business. Let's learn some of the basics of branding and how you can establish a strong brand for your new business.

# The Goals of Branding a Business

There are many opinions when it comes to what makes up a business. It can be your logo, typeface, website, and/or social media message. However, these are only things that implement your brand. Rather the brand itself is made up of the thoughts, feelings, and ideas of those associated with your company. Developing a unique brand will set you apart from the competition and give customers a reason to prefer your business over others. Branding will also encourage customers to return to you for products as long as they have a consistent and positive experience. There are four areas to consider when developing a brand:

1. The visual character of a brand is the symbol, site, and color plot.
2. The voice identity of a brand is the blog posts, mission statement, and website copy.
3. The value identity of a brand is the cause your company supports.
4. The personality identity of a brand is the culture and customer service philosophy of your company.

You can see how well branding works by asking yourself how you feel about the companies you do business with the most often. Or what do you think of when you consider your favorite drink or restaurant? Or what do you think of when you consider your cell phone company? You might have different memories and associations with each company. What makes you want to continue doing business with these companies in the long run? What do you most associate with these brands? To establish a lasting, positive brand identity for your company, you need to put yourself in the shoes of your customers.

# Why Having a Brand Is Important?

The importance of branding your business comes down to a few things. The following list shows the benefits you get from branding your business:

- Customers will have a positive memory and experience with your business. Customers will have a clear vision of your brand.
- Customers will have a clear idea of what your business stands for and values.
- You will create consistency with a brand.
- Your business will have credibility with customers.

## Defining Your Brand

Think of branding your business as a journey of self-discovery. It may be a difficult and time-consuming process, but it is well worth your time. At a minimum, you should get started by answering the following questions:

- *What is the mission of your company?*
- *What benefits and features do your products offer?*
- *What do customers and potential customers already think of your company?*
- *What qualities do you want people to associate with your company?*

This is where the research from previous steps comes in handy. You likely already know the needs, habits, and desires of your prospective customers. Defining your brand and developing a branding strategy is a complex process, even with this information. Once you've defined a brand, you need to get the word out. There are a few great ways to do this:

- Place your logo everywhere.
- Make your brand messaging and what you want to communicate.
- Integrate your brand into all aspects of your business, from how you answer the phone to how you sign emails.

- Have a voice for your company that reflects your brand, and then incorporate it into all written communication and visual imagery of your business.
- Develop a tagline for your business that is memorable, meaningful, and concise.
- Have formats and make a brand standard for your promoting materials. Everything ought to have the same color plot, symbol arrangement, and a steady see and feel.
- Make sure you follow through by delivering on your brand promise.
- Lastly, make sure you are consistent at all times. If you can't do this, then your brand will fail.

**You Need to Determine the Price of Your Soap**

When it comes to choosing a decent price to set for your soap, there are five things to consider:

- How much does it cost to make your soap?
- Can your business pay you fair wages?
- Can you afford the cost of running a business, including advertising, outsourcing, and overhead?
- Are your soaps priced to be profitable for the long haul?
- Is your pricing tested and approved by your target market?

Sometimes you'll set a cost for your cleanser; you wish to know the genuine taken a toll of making your cleanser.
This means you need to calculate the cost of materials, labor costs, and overhead expenses.

## Add Up the Cost of Supplies

Consider the typical size of soap batches you make; say you always make 50-pound blocks. Then consider what ingredients you need to make these blocks.
Make sure you price each ingredient separately and add on individual shipping. You will be confronted with having to buy

your fixings independently from different suppliers in order to urge everything you would like. When figuring your cost of goods sold, you want to be better safe than sorry. If you pick up your ingredients locally, then make sure you factor in the time and mileage cost to get supplies. Also, don't forget the cost of packaging your soap. Once you've added up the cost of supplies, then you need to also go a step further and factor in the cost of labor.

## Add Up the Cost of Labor

You wouldn't support a business that doesn't pay its employees, so why would you do the same for your business? A sustainable business needs to pay its workers a fair wage, even if the only employee is you.
Consider how long it takes you to do the entire process. This includes weighing the ingredients, melting the oils, and making the soap from start to complete product ready to be shipped.

Consider the average production at $20 an hour for minimum wage if that's what you want.
Or you can start above minimum wage. You get to set the price yourself and consider what you would pay an employee working for you. That's what you at least want to be paid yourself.

When calculating labor costs, you want to consider more than just an hourly wage. There are also the costs of benefits, payroll, and taxes. This can easily be ten to twenty percent of the hourly wage. Take your total cost of labor for the amount of time it takes to produce your typical batch of bars, then divide it by the number of bars produced to get the labor cost per bar. In fact, within the occasion that you simply don't have laborers directly, you'll arrange on expanding within the long haul. Within the occasion that ordinarily the case, you ought to twofold the brought of labor to form room inside the evaluating for enrolling laborers a short time later.

## Add Up the Cost of Overhead

Remember that when running a business, you need to spend money in order to make money. Overhead is the cost you spend to run a business. There are a lot of factors you need to consider, including rent, utilities, advertising, and more. Even if you make soaps from home, this doesn't mean you can't include the cost of rent and utilities in your overhead.

You should always include these in your pricing; you may need that in the future if you have to expand and provide your business with its own space.

Perhaps one area that many soap makers forget to account for is the cost of marketing and advertising. The rough estimate is that marketing and advertising cost about twenty percent of operating expenses during the growth phase of a business. You need to plan for these costs when pricing your soap if you ever want to expand and grow your business in the future.

You should ideally have a solid budget if you are just starting your company, and you probably already have a layout of your overhead costs. However, it can be a challenge to know exactly what costs to expect when you are just starting out your business, if you need, start with fifteen percent of your product costs and have detailed records in case you need to make adjustments to your pricing at the end of your first year in business.

A little side note is that your cost of goods sold for the purpose of pricing is going to be different than your cost of goods sold for the purpose of accounting and taxes. Figuring the cost of goods for pricing is about estimating, planning, and padding for things like extra shipping costs. However, the cost of goods for accounting and taxes means recording what you actually spend.

## Pricing Basics

Once you've established the cost per candle to make, you want to harge a little extra and consider the profit you're making. Let's say it costs you $2.98 per candle to make, so you price them at $6.00 a bar or $3 per wholesale. This still isn't much of a profit for you and your business. It is a good idea to take the costs of goods sold and multiply them by two in order to get an idea of the minimum price to set for your soap. At the least, this will give you the deepest discount you'll ever want to go to on your soap.

However, there is going to come a time as you expand and grow your business that you may find you need to increase the cost. How are you to raise your prices and keep your customers happy at the same time?

# Chapter 10

# Business Mistakes To Avoid

A candle-making company is one choice among many when you plan to establish your own work-at-home business. Starting a home business with a candle can be enjoyable and entertaining, and a way to make use of your creativity. Before you begin, though, there are several items to think about that will help secure your business success. Avoid errors that could cause the business to go bankrupt before it even begins.

## Mistake 1 - Starting without Experience

You must have at least some experience before you start, just as with any home business. You have a head start on developing a company if you've made candles as a hobby or for informal gift-giving. It would take more time to establish every business with little expertise, and it poses more risk. Only attending a workshop at a nearby community center or reading a candle-making book will give you any startup background.

## Mistake 2 - Not having a Market

Deciding when and how you should market your candle until you are official in your company is essential.

The easiest way to sell the goods is to get a website, although there are other ways too. No matter whether you market the candles, you'll need to be sure that the quality is correct, and you can attract and retain a client base and eventually generate a profit for yourself. Avoiding errors and getting fun can drive you deep into the business of producing candles.

## Mistake 3 - Not having a Research and Business Plan

A good marketing plan is a must, and much work goes hand-in-hand with that. Creating candles as a hobby or for fun is a straightforward start; it takes some preparation to move them to a business stage. You may need to explore where to buy bulk materials, including molds, candle base (whether beeswax, paraffin, gel, or soy), wicks, dyes, and oils that are scented. On the practical hand, when picking a company name and registering the company in the local city or state, you may need to prepare for the business. You'll still need a business license in some instances, even though you operate a business from your house.

## Mistake 4 - Not having a Niche

Settling on the production of candles as a commercial enterprise requires choosing a niche. If you enjoy creating a certain kind of candle and are efficient in producing, it that should be your priority. For starters, if you've made soy candles, continue with making soy candles until you're ready to expand your business, or until there's a significant financial justification for making other types of candles. The possibilities are various and broad, including floating, votive, mixed colors, unique occasions, and as well as various scents.

## Mistake 5 - Not Having a Work Space

When you want to set up a business from home, you need to make sure that you have the necessary room to support your business. You needed space to melt your candle material with a candle-making service, whatever it's that you want. You need a place to store the components of your candle; molds, pot melting, wick, and oils, etc.

You will need to be prepared to store everything you produce and to do bookkeeping and selling research in office space. Structured workspace tends to make you more effective and productive.

## Workstation Preparation

A good idea to keep your workspace safe and neat is to cover surfaces with newspaper or cardboard to protect them from any stray wax drippings that might fall. Until wax hardens, it can be difficult to see, and you don't want to return to your workspace to find the room covered in droplets of solidified wax.

When the wax has reached the right temperature to pour, you don't want to find yourself looking for containers or wicks.

Open a window or plug in an exhaust fan to make sure you have proper ventilation while working.

## Tips from the Experts

With all the DIY advice available, candle-making can seem pretty straightforward and simple, and it is, but there are some myths and misconceptions to dispel before you get started.

Many people think it's perfectly fine to use old crayons to color candle wax. Crayons weren't meant to be burned, and their odor will conflict with any enjoyment of the candle you create once you burn it. Use dyes formulated explicitly for candles.

Don't use perfume to add scent to candles.

It's another ingredient that's not mean to burn; instead, use perfume oil that's made to go well with wax. When you store your fragrance oils, make sure not to have them on a wood or metal surface.

Another myth is that you can recycle old candles by using them to make new ones. This is a bad idea. There happen to be over 300 types of wicks one can choose from, depending on the size and shape of the candle and the type of wax you're using to create it. If you mix an assortment of different waxes, odds are you're going to choose an inappropriate wick for the finished product.

You might be tempted to melt your wax in the microwave. This is a mistake because you lose the ability to monitor it. Wax needs to melt evenly, or else, it might scorch in places, and that will lend an unappealing look to your finished project. Oppositely, placing your candle in the refrigerator to speed up its setting process is a mistake.
Allowing your candle to cool down at its own pace will help ensure that the container doesn't crack and the wax doesn't shrink in places and create damp spots or tiny sinkholes. The exception to this is when you're making votive or pillar candles and need a little help prying them out of their molds, and even then, five to ten minutes at most is all you'll need.

Piling on the fragrance oil is an unnecessary waste of materials, also. Each type of wax has its own specific needs as to how much fragrance it will hold, too much, and you could end up tampering with the setting of the wax.

## Things You Should Do

Now that we've covered all of the things you should avoid while making candles, there are good practices to adapt to ensure your projects come out successfully and beautifully.

Before you discover which types of candles you enjoy best, purchase ingredients in small amounts (this is also true if you switch to a different company or supplier). A local supplier is your best choice; if you decide to make larger batches of candles in the future, shipping costs can add up.

Learn to add your fragrance oil when the wax is at the proper temperature. For soy and paraffin, it's recommended to add scent when the wax has reached between 180° and 185°F. For palm wax, those numbers are higher at 200° - 250°F.

Make sure you stir your wax consistently when it's in liquid form for at least three to five minutes. This ensures that you won't have any flaws in the finished candle and that your fragrance if you're using any, will thoroughly bind to the wax.

As mentioned above, always trim your wick, and preheat your containers. Using a thermometer is a must to know what stage your wax has reached.

Another excellent practice is to test before you commit to a project. Before you begin a batch of a dozen soy candles, make one and see how it fares. Sometimes, slight alterations in the process can help a candle burn more effectively in the end. Take notes of your tests so you can refer to them later. What should you take note of? Here's a handy list you can write on an index card:

- Date of the test
- Room temp (and humidity if you're able to find out)
- Wax type and quantity
- Additives if any
- Wick type and supplier
- Fragrances and/or dye, and how much was used
- Type of container used
- Pour temperature
- Planned cure time vs. actual cure time

On the other side of the card, record your impressions whereas the candle was lit, and any changes you'd like to form with the endeavor.

## Warnings

For general health and safety, you should make sure that you're working in a well-ventilated area when making candles. An exhaust fan and an opened window will suffice if you're unable to work in an outdoor space. As candle wax melts, it vaporizes, and this is not something you want to breathe.

You might think the kitchen is a perfect place to make candles. It can be a substitute if you don't have a separate room in which to craft, but one thing you should never do is keep your candle-making equipment there.

You might end up accidentally serving bits of wax in your food. Additionally, never pour wax down the drain of a sink. You may be thinking, "well, that's obvious," but if you pour the water from your double boiler into the sink, there might still be bits of wax in the water.

You'll be making a call to the plumber eventually if you practice this habit. As mentioned earlier in this book, never melt wax over an open flame since it is combustible. You should also always warm your containers before pouring the wax into them if they might crack (if they're made of glass, ceramic, or terracotta, for instance).

When it comes to burning candles, experts suggest leaving them lit for no more than three to four hours. Another tip you may have been unaware of, when you burn a new candle for the first time, let it burn for at least one hour. Why? Because if you burn it for too short a time, the wax will 'tunnel', leaving wax higher on the edges, and the wick sunk low.

Another tip when burning candles: trims your wicks! Trim them down to a quarter-inch before lighting to prevent carbon from building up and soot being released into the air.

Did you know that blowing out candles is the incorrect way to extinguish them? Not only will you release much smoke into the air, but the wick may drown in a pool of melted wax. Instead, use a candle snuffer. Another choice is to utilize a screwdriver to put out the candle: utilize it to begin with to tip the fire of the wick into the softened wax, and after that rectifies the wick back upright with the screwdriver.

# Chapter 11

# Promoting And Selling Your Candles Online

In your candle business, you can sell candles to individuals (retail, where you sell directly to the customer) or sell to other businesses (wholesale, where the business sells your candles to the customer) or to both.

There are advantages and disadvantages to selling directly to the customer. If you are a natural salesperson and enjoy being around other people, retail can be enjoyable.

You may already be very good at sales, or you may need to learn how to sell your candles. You can learn how to sell products by reading books, articles, and blogs on the topic. You can also attend business organizations that offer tips and help on business topics such as sales.

If you're an introvert and don't like talking to strangers, let alone trying to sell them something, retail may be a problem for you if you don't desire to learn to sell. In that case, consider hiring a salesperson.

If you sell directly to your customers, you get to keep the full price of the candle. If you sell to other businesses, they keep a percentage of the price of the candle. This may mean you need to mark up your candles more than you're comfortable with.

It may also mean selling fewer candles. However, if your candles are sold to a business that sells a large number of the candles consistently, you may come out way ahead money-wise, not to mention that you don't have to sell face-to-face to customers if you don't like selling.

## Selling Online

If you sell directly to customers, you must have a place to sell your candles. Your online shop could be a website from which you sell the candles, or it could be a situation such as Etsy.com, Amazon.com, or EBay.com.

One of the best ways you can set up an online store is by going to Wix.com; this site helps you create an online store in just a few hours, even if you have no idea how to design or set up a store.

They even offer all types of payment options for your customers, so in just a day, you can have a full-blown online candle store for under $100 a month.
To attract and bring new customers you may have to spend some money at first. One of the best ways to attract online customers is PPC (Pay per Click) advertising.

This type of advertisings is done through Google and few other search engines, but my advice would be to stay just with Google. You can also consider running Facebook ads.
The cost is pretty similar to running Google ads, but sometimes you may see better results with Facebook than Google ads.

## Social Networking Sites

This is the best way to market your products. Before you build websites or even a domain name, you should focus on marketing on sites like Facebook. For me, Facebook provided the best results, and I believe it can do the same for you too.

If you are like and don't know how social media marketing works, then hire someone from one of those sites I mentioned and let them help you. Once you see some success, then you should want to invest and get a website ready where you can display all your products and have shopping carts installed so people can buy directly from your site.

Customers want a way to contact sellers directly as well as a place where they can publicly express their shopping experiences. If you provide this, you will not only draw attention to your business, but you can also potentially increase sales. Keep in contact with your customers through networking sites such as Facebook and Twitter. Just remember to always include a link back to your website so people can find you easily.

# Chapter 12

# *Promoting And Selling Your Candles Offline*

Trends are important in any business, candle making inclusive. You must be on your toes to realize its value. Copying trends is not encouraged, but you know what it means to start a trend, recycle old ones, or keeping up with current trends. Candlemakers will always find themselves within the trend curve, and that makes it important to have some understanding of the trending issue. You can identify candle trends from within the industry and outside.

Take time and look within the industry what other candle makers are involved in so that you can come up with something more original and trendier. Take a walk around and visit the retails stores, small-town fairs, or even the international tradeshows to have insight into candle trends.
Get insight on gift items that sell around candles as well, and look out for lessons that you can learn and also integrate with making homemade candles.

You can also find inspiration from outside the industry in various forms, such as the interior design industry. You can check countless magazines, retails stores, and even TV shows that are dedicated to home interior design. Once you have identified the trends, take time and ensure that the cost, quality, and availability of raw materials used for making the candles are consistent.

You also need to look at the capability of selling the finished product at a price that's competitive and how you can select your ideal market. You should also look at the consumer's acceptance of the safe use of your homemade candles.

Ensure that you include candle burning instructions that can assist customers that lack sufficient knowledge about the candles. Assure customers that there are no flammable products used in the candle's burning area. Let them also be aware of how the candle might perform under different scenarios. Customers should know that your candles meet all the necessary safety criteria.

The homemade candles that you make should be able to compete in different markets regardless of the size or background of the business.

## Marketing and selling in local stores

You can start out by providing the best service to the local stores such as the local gift shops, homes, and any other place within the local market. Once you can prove to them that you can deliver quality candles; they will be willing to buy from you since they will also be saving on freight charges. You can also make arrangements with the local stores so that you can as well track their inventory level. Look out for the local craft, and art shows as such are good starting points where locals can get to show interest in your products.

## Fundraisers and local organizations

Fundraisers and local organizations frequently provide the right place for selling homemade candles. It's great because you get to receive payments immediately as you deliver. Fundraisers provide you with the opportunity to also build your company within the ommunity, and people will still be interested in buying candles from you even after the events are over.

One good thing about making candles is the fact that there isn't any wrong or right way of making them.

You should note, however, the emphasis on the cost of materials used so that it doesn't end up diminishing your returns.

Sometimes it's the fragrance or the decoration that sells the candles, so remember to add scents that many within your target market find to be appealing.

## Marketing based on seasons

You can try marketing your candles based on the seasons as it helps in developing a sustained market all year round. You can use fragrances that appeal to the given seasons. For effective marketing, ensure that you do the following:

- Make products of excellent quality regarding appearance and safety.
- You should also be able to sell at competitive prices.
- Develop products with a wide range of fragrances or new products.
- Ensure that you develop a solid reputation for your business.
- Be aware of your marketplace and the limitations.
- Keep the material costs under control.

## Expand product offering

The candle market has become quite competitive, and the retailers are more price sensitive to various types of candles. One way that you can use to create a new market for your homemade candles is by expanding your product offering, as that may assist in growing your business. Not only will you be able to improve your market within the existing customers, but you will also be able to increase your demand amongst those who were not initially buying from you.

The new product line can be something like having a range of fragrances, filling new containers, or even having an edge for essential oils, amongst other things. You can also expand your line by exploring making other new types of candles. These could be candles of different kinds of wax such as gel candles and such like.

## Consult with companies that sell costly products

You can build a relationship with big companies that sell expensive products and work on providing them with samples that they can give away as a gift with purchases. Your target should be creating a relationship with them that can lead to future sales. You can add some additional utility, such as putting a bottom that's protective to avoid damage to furniture. You can also make the candles easy to light.

## Gifts

Giving out candles as gifts to colleagues and family is a good way to create awareness about your business. Make sure you also encourage them to help in marketing your products.

# Chapter 13

# Selling Candles To Gift Shops

## Selling in Retail Stores

Another possibility for some is to sell in retail stores. Whether this is a retail space of your own or selling products in an established store, the advantages and disadvantages are largely the same.

Selling in your own retail space often requires you to establish a customer base in order to have success. Often those who sell from their own retail space started at local community events or online in order to develop loyal customers first. If you aren't ready to sell products from your own retail store, you can start by selling from an established retail space.

When choosing possible locations for selling your products, it is important to do some research. You should find a store that has a similar aesthetic to the products you're offering. This ensures you are attracting customers who already shop for similar items inside the store. You'll also want to find out more about the company.

Consider asking the following questions when doing your research:

- *How long has the business been open?*

- *Does the business have multiple locations?*

- *Are they already selling similar items?*

- *What advertising and social media presence does the business have?*

It is also important to consider other factors that may help your products sell. Does the business have loyal customers and a strong social media presence? You should also consider how your products may help the store since you are essentially entering into a selling partnership with the business, and you need to bring something to the table as well.

Once you've identified a list of local stores you want to work with, you need to approach them to make the sale. When you sell in a retail store, they'll be doing half of the work for you when it comes to advertising, selling, and displaying the product. However, you won't have a lot of control over where and how your products are positioned. The person in the store may not be educated about your products and may not be able to sell your product effectively to potential customers.

One of the main disadvantages of selling in a retail space is that it will require wholesale pricing, which is often about fifty percent of your retail pricing. As a new business, most forget to factor in all the costs of doing business and price their products too low. This means you may not be able to afford the fifty percent discount when starting your business. However, if you can reduce your costs and make your production process as efficient as possible, then you might be able to reach that price point.

To summarize:

## Advantages

1. You'll spend less time selling products, so you'll have more time to make products.
2. You have an access to an already established customer base.

## Disadvantages

1. Wholesale pricing may not be something a new business startup can afford.
2. You won't have control of merchandising.
3. You won't be able to represent the product yourself.

Once you have an idea of where to sell your product, you'll need to finalize your products for sale. First step is to ensure you have professional-looking soaps to sell.

# *Chapter 14*

# *Weekly Plan To Start Your Business*

**Dream, plan, go!**

Here is a simple weekly plan for your candle-making business that you can follow. See the sample table below. These are the days that you should do certain tasks, and how long they will take. Do this every week for a month, and then evaluate your progress.

This weekly plan can also be used as an ongoing record of your business activity. You can see how much business you have done so far this year, what products or services you sell most often, even where you spend most of your time in your business. It is sometimes called a "dashboard" in business.

In this table you see how many hours you should work each day, and on which days. For example, Tuesday morning is your "educational" day. You should find out as much as you can about candle-making and other related arts. At least two hours are required for the classroom activity, plus two more hours in the business office or studio where you work.

The rest of the time is for other things, such as marketing, or selling, or developing your product line. You want to be well prepared to sell your products and services to customers.

This weekly chart assumes that you have a small business with 5 employees. You will also need a daily chart like the one on page 6 for the actual working hours you see on your payroll records.
You can use this weekly chart in many different ways, and it will help you keep track of how fast your business is growing. It will provide perspective on how much time you are actually spending doing work and not just wishing you were in business.

If you are active in other businesses besides candle making, you can use this chart to keep track of the time you spend each week in each business.

Keep a copy of this chart on your computer or on a file. You can update it each week by typing in the new information after the old information is copied over from the previous week. Some people put the entire weekly chart into their computer and update it each week.

This chart can be used to show that you have a business, and to prove that you are capable of doing a job. If necessary, such as when seeking a loan or applying for assistance from a government agency, you can show this chart to demonstrate that you are committed to your business. You will find it useful when applying for bank loans and seeking other types of financing.

If you are using this chart to support a claim for disability or other forms of public assistance, be sure to keep a copy of the chart, and any supporting documents. As you go along and make progress in your business, you can adjust the table to suit your needs. You may add more tasks or subtract old ones.

The sample table below will give you an idea of how it all fits together with your business and other activities. The sample table is just one format for the same information, but it is suggested that you use a computer spreadsheet program like Microsoft Excel for maximum flexibility in creating charts and tables when making changes. If you do not have office software yet, consider using word processing software instead.

# ACTION PLAN

**WELCOMING AND CARING**

| ACTION REQUIRED | STRATEGIC LINK0 | WHO WILL DO THIS? | BY WHEN? | WHERE WILL IT BE REPORTED? |
|---|---|---|---|---|
|  |  |  |  |  |
|  |  |  |  |  |
|  |  |  |  |  |

**WELL ORGANISED AND CALM**

| ACTION REQUIRED | STRATEGIC LINK0 | WHO WILL DO THIS? | BY WHEN? | WHERE WILL IT BE REPORTED? |
|---|---|---|---|---|
|  |  |  |  |  |
|  |  |  |  |  |
|  |  |  |  |  |

**INFORMATIVE**

| ACTION REQUIRED | STRATEGIC LINK0 | WHO WILL DO THIS? | BY WHEN? | WHERE WILL IT BE REPORTED? |
|---|---|---|---|---|
|  |  |  |  |  |
|  |  |  |  |  |
|  |  |  |  |  |

**GENERAL POINTS**

| ACTION REQUIRED | STRATEGIC LINK0 | WHO WILL DO THIS? | BY WHEN? | WHERE WILL IT BE REPORTED? |
|---|---|---|---|---|
|  |  |  |  |  |
|  |  |  |  |  |
|  |  |  |  |  |

## NOTES

_____

_____

# Candle Making
# BUDGET

| ITEM | BUDGET | ACTUAL | VAR | VAR % |
|---|---|---|---|---|
| Fixtures and equipment | | | | |
| Decorating and remodeling | | | | |
| Installation charges | | | | |
| Starting inventory | | | | |
| Deposits | | | | |
| Licenses and permits | | | | |
| Cash | | | | |
| Other | | | | |
| **Total Start-Up Costs** | | | | |

# Candle Making
# BUDGET

DATES _____ TO _____

| ITEM | BUDGET | ACTUAL | VAR | VAR % |
|---|---|---|---|---|
| Waxes and gels | | | | |
| Wicks | | | | |
| Molds | | | | |
| Dyes | | | | |
| Scents | | | | |
| Additives | | | | |
| Mold release agent | | | | |
| Measuring instruments | | | | |
| Packaging materials | | | | |
| Melting pots | | | | |
| **Total Supply Costs** | | | | |

# Candle Making
# BUDGET

DATES          TO

| ITEM | BUDGET | ACTUAL | VAR | VAR % |
|------|--------|--------|-----|-------|
| Insurance | | | | |
| Transportation | | | | |
| Office & operational supplies | | | | |
| Shipping | | | | |
| Depreciation | | | | |
| Interest | | | | |
| Research and development | | | | |
| Other | | | | |
| **Total Administrative Expenses** | | | | |

# Candle Making
# BUDGET

DATES _____ TO _____

| ITEM | BUDGET | ACTUAL | VAR | VAR % |
|---|---|---|---|---|
| Television | | | | |
| Radio | | | | |
| Internet Ads | | | | |
| Newspaper | | | | |
| Email | | | | |
| Social media | | | | |
| Direct mail | | | | |
| Magazines | | | | |
| Trade shows | | | | |
| Print | | | | |
| **Total Mkt and Ads Expense** | | | | |

# Candle Making
# BUDGET

DATES _____ TO _____

| ITEM | BUDGET | ACTUAL | VAR | VAR % |
|------|--------|--------|-----|-------|
| Lease or mortgage | | | | |
| Telephone | | | | |
| Other utilities | | | | |
| Repairs and maintenance | | | | |
| Other | | | | |
| **Total Facilities Expenses** | | | | |

# Candle Making
# BUDGET

DATES          TO

| ITEM | BUDGET | ACTUAL | VAR | VAR % |
|---|---|---|---|---|
| Payroll | | | | |
| Payroll taxes | | | | |
| Other payroll expenses | | | | |
| Professional service fees | | | | |
| Contract labor | | | | |
| Other | | | | |
| **Total Labor Expense** | | | | |
| Income taxes | | | | |
| Property taxes | | | | |
| Other (specify) | | | | |
| **Total Tax Expenses** | | | | |

# Candle Making
# BUDGET

DATES                    TO

## Total Expenses

| ITEM | BUDGET | ACTUAL | VAR | VAR % |
|------|--------|--------|-----|-------|
| Sales Revenue | | | | |
| Other Revenue | | | | |

## Total Revenue

**Total Revenue**  **Total Expenses**

=

**Net Profit / Loss**

# Conclusion

After reading this book about the candle-making business, I hope that you know how to make candles at home. The book gives some guidance that is quite relevant to the candle-making business in general. This article would only have some topics which relate to candle making business.

Firstly, you need to learn what type of wax you want to make candles from. You can choose paraffin wax, soy wax, beeswax, or gel candles. There are advantages and disadvantages to each type of wax that you should know before you make this decision. If you are not going to be making huge quantities of candles, paraffin wax is likely for you. In this case, you will need to learn how to make paraffin wax.

Secondly, you need to know what color tones you want the candles to have. Many different colors and combinations of colors can be achieved by mixing dyes with molten wax. The more of these colors you use, the brighter your candles will look, but at the expense of a higher price per candle.

Thirdly, if you are going to make candles in greater quantities than one or two dozen, it will be useful to know how much wax is needed for each candle.

For something like a three-tier wedding cake, it works out that around 5 lbs. (2 kg) of wax is needed for each of the tiers.

Fourthly, you need to know what type of wicks to use in the candles. Every wick has a different purpose, and there is a wide range of types available. Scented candles always have a cotton wick because they can tolerate the extra heat generated by the scent oils. This means that you can leave your candles for longer before they burn right down.

Fifthly, you need to decide on what color glassware you want to put your candles in. Then you need to select from among all the various styles of containers and containers of all sizes. Some people prefer clear or colored glass, which can be obtained by using colored glass rods or sheets with clear glass rods or sheets.

Sixthly, you need to know what type of label you want to put on the bottles or jars where you will be storing your finished candles. There are both printable and sticker labels available. The printable labels tend to look nicer and are easier to use, but they don't last as long as sticker labels. I would recommend that you try the printable labels first because they require a small amount of additional time in preparation, but well worth it when your candles are ready for sale.

Seventhly, there is one final thing that will help when selling candles at candle shows or on the internet; it is essential to know how much wax you will need for each candle. This can be estimated with the help of a spreadsheet. You will need to know the size of your candles, the color mix and type of wick you are using, as well as the weight of your containers.

Lastly, if you make candles from paraffin wax, remember this; paraffin wax is extremely flammable. You should not leave your candles unattended unless they are in their container or on top of properly vented shelves or racks. Make sure that they are covered whenever you are not in the room and keep fires safely extinguished at all times.

And make sure that when you like to start your own business in candle-making, you should always remember the safe and well procedure of starting the business, like keeping fire extinguishers around the candle-making area. I hope that this book gave you a lot of ideas before starting your own business in candle making.

CPSIA information can be obtained
at www.ICGtesting.com
Printed in the USA
LVHW061112130621
690110LV00020B/526